My First Book About Bears

Amazing Animal Books

Children's Picture Books

By Molly Davidson

Mendon Cottage Books

JD-Biz Publishing

I0422862

Read More Amazing Animal Books

Purchase at Amazon.com

Table of Contents

Introduction

When you first hear about the animal, a bear, you may think that they are big and mean. But actually, bears are gentle animals. They are social and playful too.

About Bears

Mother bears will fight anything that tries to hurt her cubs, which means her babies. Mothers will even fight dads away, if they feel like they are harmful!

Bears are very good at climbing and running really fast.

They also know how to swim, this is how they are able to catch fish to eat.

Features of Bears

Bears are big, covered in fur, have large noses, short tails, and sharp chewing teeth.

Bears see as well as humans, but they only see in black and white.

A bear's hearing is 100 times better than a humans. Bears can hear lots of sounds that humans cannot.

Where Bears Live

Most bears live in the forest, except polar bears, they live in the arctic.

Bears usually live in caves, this way they are protected when they sleep all winter.

What Bears Eat

Bears eat more plants than they do meat.

When they eat meat, it is smaller, warm blooded, animals.

A tiger is about the only animal that will try to eat a bear alive, other animals will eat them if they are dead.

Behavior and Vocalization

Bears are active most of the day, some people think they are active only at night, which is not true.

Bears communicate through body language, sounds, and scents.

Bears usually travel by themselves, except a mother and her new baby cubs.

Asiatic Black Bear

These bears are found in Iran, Afghanistan, Bangladesh, India, China, and other Asian countries.

The scientific name of the Asiatic Black Bear means the 'Moon bear of the Tibet'.

They eat honey, fruits, berries, beetle larvae, nuts, and carrion (rotten dead flesh of an animal).

Some Asiatic black bears hibernate (sleep all winter), but most live in a warm place, so they can stay awake all winter.

Black Bear

The most common bear in the World is the black bear.

Black Bears have big ears, sharp claws that are curved and help them in climbing trees

This bear eats grass, nuts, insects, fish, rodents, moose, berries, and deer.

Black bears live from 21 to 33 years.

Brown Bear

There are so many different kinds of brown bear that it is called "The bear with too any names."

Brown bears live in the wilderness and national parks in the Rocky Mountains in Wyoming, Idaho, Montana, and Washington.

Grizzly Bears, a type of brown bear, have a large hump on their shoulder.

Brown bears eat mice, roots of plants, animal meat and the carcass (skeleton), and grasses of all kinds.

Panda Bear

Panda bears are found in China and are disappearing because humans are taking over where they live.

Pandas eat stems, leaves, bamboo, and meat, if they can find it.

Pandas do not eat enough fat to hibernate (sleep all winter), so they just move in the winter to where it is warm.

Red Panda Bear

Pandas like to be by themselves, they like to rest and be lazy.

Pandas are on the endangered list, which means not very many of them are left on the planet today.

Polar Bear

Polar bears, also known as 'Sea Bears', are the largest of all the bears.

They live in the Arctic Circle, in the arctic circle, more than half the polar bears live in Canada.

Polar bears have black skin, that helps keep them warm by the sun, and white fur.

Their paws are webbed to help them swim. Certain spots on their feet are not covered in fur and are rough to help them from slipping on the ice.

Polar Bears eat seals and other water animals or birds.

Sloth Bear

Sloth bears look different very from other bears and are very calm. They sometime are confused for the animal, sloth, because they look alike.

These bears in the warm and wet forests of South East Asia, Nepal, Bangladesh, and Burma.

They have no front teeth and have a long tongue and fat lips so they can suck termites from dirt hills.

These bears are awake at night and sleep during the day.

They like to be alone and are excellent climbers of trees.

Spectacled Bear

The eyes of these bears have light colored rings around them making it appear like they're wearing glasses (spectacles) and that is how they get their name as 'Spectacled Bears'.

Spectacled Bear is also known as the Andean Bear because they are found only in the Andes mountains in South America.

These bears eat meat, plants, but they love fruit trees and could be seen eating and sleeping for days in fruit trees.

Sun Bear

Sun Bear is the smallest of all bears.

They live in hot and wet areas, living in trees, eating fruits and insects.

Sun Bears have thick fur that helps protect them from mud, insects, and dirt.

Something neat about the sun bear is they have long tongues so they can get extra honey from the bee hives.

Sun bears are also on the endangered list.

Bears and Humans

Bears are shy and avoid humans most of the time.

If the bear cubs feel threatened, mother bears behave very mean and will attack.

Where bears get in trouble with humans is when they attack livestock (cows, sheep, horses) or try to eat their crops.

Myths and Legends

Most tribes worshipped bears because of their amazing fishing and hunting skills.

Siberian people thought bears to be the spirit of their forefathers. Koreans also think bears are their ancestors.

The national animal of Finland is the bear.

A fairy tale of Russia speaks of a boy named Ivan who tries to kill a mother bear and her cubs. He was punished by having his head turned into a bear's head and was never allowed to live in his village again.

Koreans identify bears as symbolic animals and consider them to be their ancestors.

Bears are worshipped in early China and in Ainu cultures. In the Alpine zone, stories about saints taming bears are common.

Our books are available at

1. Amazon.com

2. Barnes and Noble

3. Itunes

4. Kobo

5. Smashwords

6. Google Play Books

Download Free Books!

http://MendonCottageBooks.com

Publisher

JD-Biz Corp

P O Box 374

Mendon, Utah 84325

http://www.jd-biz.com/

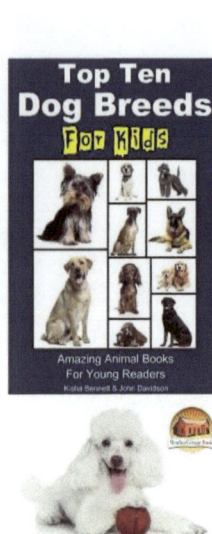

Top Ten Dog Breeds For Kids
Amazing Animal Books For Young Readers
Kristal Bennett & John Davidson

German Shepherds
Dog Books for Kids
K. Bennett

Bulldogs
Dog Books for Kids
K. Bennett

Dachshund
Dog Books for Kids
K. Bennett

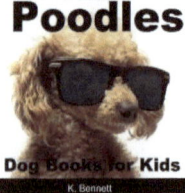

Poodles
Dog Books for Kids
K. Bennett

Labrador Retrievers
Dog Books for Kids
K. Bennett

Rottweilers
Dog Books for Kids
K. Bennett

Boxers
Dog Books for Kids
K. Bennett

Golden Retrievers
Dog Books for Kids
K. Bennett

Puppies
Dog Books For Kids
Amazing Animal Books
By John Davidson

Beagles
Dog Books for Kids
K. Bennett

Yorkshire Terriers
Dog Books for Kids
K. Bennett

Cats For Kids
Amazing Animal Books For Young Readers
K. Bennett & John Davidson

Dogs
Top Ten Dog Breeds For Kids
Amazing Animal Books For Young Readers
Zahra Jazeel & John Davidson

Foxes For Kids
Amazing Animal Books For Young Readers
Zahra Jazeel & John Davidson

Wolves For Kids
Amazing Animal Books For Young Readers
By John Davidson and Virginia Fidler